10 STEPS TO HEALING FROM NARCISSISTIC ABUSE

By:

Noraima Y. Torres

Dedication

This book is dedicated to my two beautiful children Nicole and Giovanni, who have shown me what unconditional love is. Who have given me the strength and hope to continue bettering myself and continue living. Who have motivated me enough to change and recover from my own Codependency. I love you both more than words could ever say. I also want to dedicate this book to all of you who have or still are struggling from abusive relationships to a narcissist. I too have been where you are and I want you to know that there is a life full of love and peace on the other side of this pain. You are no longer a victim. You are a survivor and you can and will be happy again.

Introduction

You think your life is finally coming together perfectly. Everything seems like a dream come true. You have met the love of your life and you are absolutely sure of this. You get butterflies in your stomach, you are glowing. They tell you that they have never met anybody like you, that this is destiny, that they are your soulmate. They introduce you to their friends and family. You begin to feel like you are on cloud 9. Then one day things change a little. You have your first argument. Surely, all couples argue at one point or another, but this is different. They begin to verbally attack you, calling you worthless, blaming you for everything that has gone wrong. You are left wondering what the hell just happened. They go out and cheat, or even worse, they sleep with their ex. You are destroyed and devastated left to wonder what just happened and is it your fault? All of a sudden they come back. Begging you to take them back. Telling you how much he loves you and how he can't live without you. You miss them so much. The pain feels unbearable. How are you ever going to live without him? So you decide to give him another chance. After all it really was the first time he treated you this way and let's face it he was a little drunk that time. You have mad passionate makeup sex, things go back to normal. You are feeling happy again and everything seems to be going pretty smoothly. But little by little you begin to realize that the promises he made when you took him back are not being taken into action. Every argument leads to a full on verbal attack. Constant name calling and making you feel worthless. So you begin to blame yourself. You begin to think you are going crazy. It must be your jealousy or insecurity that makes him act so angry with you. You actually have become paranoid, suspicious and jealous. You keep wondering what's wrong with you.

If these scenarios sound familiar, brace yourself because you have just encountered a Narcissist. Forget everything you ever knew about bad relationships. These relationships will shake the very core of your existence and after this encounter you will never be the same. But you can and you will recover. Even if right now you cannot see the light at the end of the tunnel, you will in time. Narcissistic abuse is one of the most unnoticed and yet most damaging forms of abuse that exist. The typical Narcissist follows a very distinct pattern of Idealize, Devalue and Discard phases. These phases will leave you feeling like you have lost your mind but you have to trust that you have not. The last and final phase where the narcissist Discards you is typically the hardest phase to deal with. We are left with so many unanswered questions. So many doubts. Wondering if we caused everything. If it's our fault. If only we had done x, y or z. But the truth is that it is not our fault and you did not cause this person to be a narcissist or verbally abusive to you. There is nothing you can do to change this person, or make this person stop abusing you. A Narcissistic Personality disorder is a personality disorder in which a person is excessively preoccupied with personal adequacy, power, prestige and vanity. Mentally unable to see the destructive damage they are causing themselves or others. It is a Cluster B Personality Disorder. And you cannot cure it. You cannot change it. And you did not cause it. The only thing you can do is create a new life for yourself, and eventually move on from this horrific experience. But moving on is not an easy task. And letting go is even harder. But your life depends on it. Starting today, you must take control back of your life and decide to live.

Before I jump into the steps to healing, I want to take a moment to share with you my story. My name is Noraima Torres and I lived with my narcissistic ex for 2 years. I didn't always know my ex was a narcissist. I must add that my ex was a female but that narcissists can be both genders. This relationship began at lightning speed. But there was such a strong connection between us in my head, in my heart I knew she was the one. We both came from very different backgrounds. I was a single mother struggling to just get by on my own with my children. My ex was also a mother but living alone and partying every night with her friends. We both had a different set of priorities in life. My priority was family and living a quiet peaceful life with my children. Her priority was making sure she was admired and always the center of attention of her friends. We began dating and after our first week together she went out with friends and I had to work overnight. I came home at 3am from work and fell asleep. She had been trying to reach me but I had fallen asleep. When I woke up the next morning I woke up to a bunch of emails and text messages from her calling me every name in the book. Put downs of the worst kind. I immediately called her and said I was done, that I was not going to be talked to that way. Immediately, she apologized and justified it as her being out drunk with friends. She said she got that way only when she drank whisky and that she would lay off the whisky. I believed that promise and decided to ignore the giant red flag waving in my face. That was the beginning of a 2 year verbally abusive narcissistic relationship. Little did I know that this was her go to coping skill for arguments. Making me feel worthless somehow gave her a feeling of grandiosity. Something was not right here, but surely it had to be my fault because she said so. So two months passed and her lease was coming to an end. Of course myself being the codependent that I was at the time, I immediately offered to let her come live with me so that we would not have to live far apart. She had said that once her lease was over she would have to move about an hour away with family. So I was terrified of distance breaking us up and I asked her to come live with me. Hell, I even paid for the U-Haul truck, helped her move everything, and even carried her ginormous mattress on my back. This was the beginning of our new life together, I was going to have everything I had always wanted. Love, family, stability and someone to share my life with. Things were rocky from the moment we started living together. She had a lot of female friends but the most disturbing factor was that she had slept with almost all of her female friends. Being a codependent, I became afraid of getting hurt by her right away.

Especially since all of these friends were people she was intimate with. But she had a huge desire to receive attention from these friends. I tried to be more understanding and even tried to become friends with them in order to keep her happy. But I noticed that this was not enough for her. She did not want me present when she wanted to hang out with these people. So this would cause a lot of arguments because I asked myself over and over why does my presence bother her? Why does she not want me there? The feeling of rejection and fear of abandonment took control of me and lead me to my own Codependent Catastrophe. I did not trust her. Something deep down inside of me could not trust that she would not hurt me. A lot of it had to do with my codependency I will admit that having lived through abuse as a child really has affected my ability to trust others and has given me a fear of abandonment like no other. Either way something did not seem right.

August of 2014 I received an email from her old room-mate whom she owed money to. In this email her room-mate decides to air my ex's dirty laundry. She said that she did not want to tell me but that I seemed like a really nice girl and that she did not think what my ex was doing was right. She said that the entire time we began dating, my ex was still sleeping with her ex. It honestly felt like a bullet to my chest. Words can't even explain the pain I felt when I read these words. So I asked my ex, and I really wanted her to be honest with me. So I begged, I pleaded, I made compromises. Anything to just get her to tell me the truth. I would have to say about 6 hours passed that day of nothing but my ex denying everything the room-mate said. Finally I said to her, look we have a better chance of making this work if you can just tell me the truth. And so she did. She admitted to having slept with her ex but justified it that it was just the start of our relationship and that she didn't know where things were going with us so it didn't really count as cheating. I immediately told her to leave that I needed to think about things. That whole night she would not stop calling and texting begging me to forgive her. She said she loved me and wanted to make this work that it would never happen again. She swore it would never happen again. It didn't even take a full 24 hours when I had already welcomed her back home with open arms. But this time, I had questions.

I wanted to know everything and how it happened. I wanted to know why her ex. I wanted to know if she thought her ex was prettier or skinnier or had more money than me. My self-esteem was gone. Completely. I was walking around questioning her every move and terrified of when this was going to happen again. I never really felt like she really regretted hurting me the way she did. And no matter how many times I tried to explain to her how bad she hurt me, she didn't get it. So from that point on I became even more doubtful of her and questioned her, gave her ultimatums, checked her phone, emails and made myself sick of worry in the process. My codependent behaviors had reached a new level and had taken control of my life. I was sick. I was scared. Terrified of her doing this to me again. And my worst fear came back to life.

At this point we were constantly arguing. Most of the time we were going out to visit her friends or family about an hour away in her hometown. These events usually lead to drinking and I'm not talking about a casual Margarita on a sunny day. I'm talking about my ex drinking a 24 case of Corona all by herself and getting shit faced drunk. The problem we were having here was that I was the designated driver. Of course because there was no way my ex could drive after all that alcohol so I had to be the adult all the time.

She would want to leave her friend's house with beer and alcohol in her pockets because 24 beers obviously was not enough. This would cause huge arguments on the long ride home. She would start calling me names which was always the first resort. Then she would start accusing me of cheating, having a back-up plan, doing her dirty, lying to her and then tell me I was not worthy or that I was just a scandalous whore. She always hit below the belt. To top that off let me explain my car ride with her. She would start screaming at me and tell me to pull over the car or she was going to jump out. I would pull over and she would start running in another direction on the highway, or she would sit near the highway with her beer in hand. But I was always the bad one because I made her act this way she said. If I wasn't so jealous and crazy she would never act this way. So I believed it.

So after many fights like this October came along. The week before Halloween we had an argument about a Halloween party we were both planning on going to together. Well during the argument she made it clear that she did not want me there. That I was a burden. And that she did not have fun when I was there. So I told her to leave and go have fun. She packed all her belongings and left. I was devastated because I really did love her and I really missed her. Even though now when I look back at this I don't know what exactly I was missing. So about two days after she left, she shows up at my apartment with a ring in hand. Mind you, it was a very cheap department store ring but still it was the thought that counted or so I thought. She got on her knees and asked me to forgive her, that she couldn't live without me and that she wanted to marry me. So I told her I was going to think about it and let her know this time. Frankly at this point I was exhausted from all the fighting. I decided to email her best friend who was also another girl she had slept with who had a huge problem with my ex being with me. We had previously had a falling out so I tried to make peace with her best friend and emailed her and said Look (my ex) and I are going to get married and I really want us to get along because I know how much you mean to her. Immediately her friend responded, lol I guess she forgot to tell you she spent the night and slept with her ex again this weekend. Threw it in my face. I couldn't even believe it. The one thing my ex promised she did again. So I sent my ex a message and she did not respond to absolutely anything I had to say. Ignored everything I had to say. I was blown away because this was somebody who had just come to my home and asked me to marry her that very same morning.

About a week passed and I had decided I was going to do something nice for myself since I had been feeling so horrible lately. So I went to the beauty salon and got my hair done and died it red. Deep down it was an effort to please my ex and get her back because I knew she loved red headed women. So I posted some new pictures online and sure enough, the text messages and phone calls started all over again. I was not responding to anything. So she decided to show up at my house. I did not give in. I was furious and I made sure she knew I meant business. So after numerous attempts on her end she finally got me in a weak moment and asked to take me to dinner to talk. She confessed that she had only slept with her ex because her ex always made it easy and that she was not a real woman like me but just an easy lay. And that she was looking for me in someone else. Whatever. But at the time I believed it. I took her back yet again. And ignored all the red flags slapping me in the face. We spent the holidays together basically doing everything she wanted and me riding along just to keep her happy. But the fights continued and the insults became a daily event. I hated the fact that she had to call me names to make herself feel

better. I really tried to understand why she called me these horrible

things. She would apologize and say it would never happen again.

But it always did happen again. And no matter how much she saw

me cry or how bad I said it hurt me, she would not stop. She could

not stop. At that point I started researching verbal abuse online and

joined a support group to find someone to speak to that could tell

me if I was really losing my mind. I had lost my will to live. I started

to believe everything she said to me, especially when she said that

her verbal abuse was justified because I was crazy and jealous. And

that I made her act this way. The more I researched verbal abuse

the more I understood what was going on. I never imagined in a

million years that I would be abused in a relationship this way. I

never imagined verbal abuse was real. But it was very real and

staring at me in the face.

February 2015

Another drunken party at her friend's house. At this point we were

struggling not only in the relationship but financially as well. We were living at a hotel for a while due to financial hardships and just really not being able to get our shit together, together. So as we left the party she was already drunk as ever. I drove us home. Our children were in the car, including her daughter. She decides she wants to continue drinking and tells me to stop at a gas station so she can buy more beer. I told her no that we only had $10 left to our name for the entire week. And she really did not seem to care that we were broke whatsoever. So she gets out of the car and runs into the gas station and brings back beer. I tried to grab the beer away because the kids were in the car watching her. So she decides to run out of my car yet again, like a toddler and run and run, beer in hand yet her daughter in my car watching everything. Like the true codependent doormat I was, I decide to go after her in my car, screaming out the window begging her to get back into the car. She was literally throwing a tantrum. A 31 yr old woman throwing a tantrum outside a gas station because she wanted beer. So I called her mother because desperate times call for desperate measures right? So now I have her mother on speaker phone yelling at my ex to get back in the car. So she finally gets back in the car. We go back to the hotel and the kids get out and go inside to sleep. Meanwhile my ex and I stay in the car, still arguing about her inability to put us first and understand that we needed the money for food or gas instead of beer. All of sudden my ex decides to pour an entire 16oz can of beer in my face, directly in my eyes. I was blinded for a few minutes and then all hell broke loose. I was fed up~ We started hitting each other and manually fighting each other in the car at 4am. Screaming and I know deep down that it is never ok to hit someone. But I had enough that day. After we were done fighting my ex says to me, you are garbage and you're nothing but a slut. You are worthless and even worse she said…You are a nasty lay. That was a really low blow and I was really just left in shock when someone who said they loved me, and loved being intimate with me tells me that I was terrible in bed and that I was nasty. It really hurt and at that moment I knew things were never going to be the same again. I walked out of the car and went inside and just sat there staring at the wall wondering what on earth I ever did so wrong to make her hate me so much. She tried to apologize and promise it would never happen again. But I was in shock and I was numb. I really felt that this person hated me.

May 2015-

The week of Mother's day came around and here we were still fighting on a daily basis. Things were bad. The verbal attacks were getting worse. We tried couples therapy for a while but that became too expensive and during our arguments everything the therapist said to us went right out the window. So we had yet another huge fight and my ex decided to leave. She was constantly complaining about how she was a caged prisoner and that she wanted to go party with her friends and I did not want to be with someone who felt like a prisoner with me. I was fed up at this point. So I let her go. A week passed and then another week passed. And then she began texting and calling. At this point I knew she had already slept with her ex. I had actually found out through a mutual friend. I had lost all respect for her. I tried to numb the pain but looking for a human band aid. I met someone and became intimate with them myself. Just once. But I realized quickly that I still missed my ex and I could not get over her. I wanted my ex to feel the pain she made me feel every single time she would go sleep with her ex. But she didn't feel pain. She had no heart. Yet, I could not let her go. It was like I was addicted to her. I really was. Like an addict seeking a fix. I needed my ex to love me or pretend again. It was sick toxic codependent dance. I didn't realize I was dancing with a narcissist. I started to research more on abuse and I came across a Narcissist Support group online. And wow I was left speechless when every single thing she had done to me had a definition and explanation. But I still was not ready to let go. So I responded to her messages. And I told her we were not going to work out because we had both slept with someone else at that point. She denied sleeping with her ex or anybody and let me believe that I was the only one who did something wrong. I agreed to meet her in a parking lot and we talked for about 8 hours that day. In my car, for that long. I told her about the girl I messed around with to numb my pain. And she did everything she could to make me feel terrible about it. And so I asked her numerous times, did you sleep with you ex again? The answer was no. So I decided to put everything behind us and start over. We had an amazing night together making up. I thought finally things are going to get better between us. There is hope after all.

The next day I could not sit with the feeling I had in my gut that she was lying to me about her ex. So I tested out my theory. I emailed her ex and told her we were getting back together and that my ex denied seeing her this time. The next thing I know her ex sends me a picture of my ex lying in her bed, naked. On Mother's day. I could not believe it. Again. With the same person. I drove to my ex's job and told her we needed to talk. She came into the car and begged me to forgive her, that she loved me but that she was scared to tell me because things were going so well she did not want to lose me. But here's the thing. If I came out on my own and told her about the one night stand I had, why could she not be honest with me? Why was honesty impossible for her? After an entire day of arguing and her forcing herself into the apartment. I was exhausted. I was drained. I was numb. And I took her back again. She contacted her ex and told her that she was done for good this time, that I was the only one she ever loved. I truly believed that this time it was over. She proposed to me and asked me to marry her. I wanted to start over with her and pretend like the past year never happened. I wanted her to stop insulting me. I wanted her to love me and to only want to be with me. I wanted to be the only woman for her. I wanted to make her happy. So on May 25 I married her. To think that things were going to get better or that marriage makes a toxic relationship better is a huge mistake. Every single day from the moment we got married was disastrous. Things never got better. She insulted me every single day and night. I could not get her to stop no matter what I did. I remember that I became so depressed from her verbal abuse that I laid in bed night after night emailing my best friend telling her how I wanted to die and how I did not want to live like this anymore. That my marriage had already fallen apart when it had just started. My codependency was at rock bottom and I had no idea how to fix this, how to fix myself or how to leave her because I couldn't. I felt stuck. And I blamed myself for everything. My friend said something to me that has stuck with me since then. She said, you know you are not stuck, you don't have to stay married to her. You can get out. At the time I didn't think I had this choice. But today I know that I do.

July 2015- We were out at a bar and drove home arguing the whole ride. We got pulled over because my ex was speeding and she ended up getting arrested that night for driving with a suspended license. So as she is getting arrested I asked the officer to let her know that I needed her cell phone in order to contact her family so they can help me bail her out of jail. She tells the officer no. This woman refused to leave me her phone saying that she needed something on there. The biggest red flag was waving in my face and I decided to ignore it. Deep into my codependency I pawned everything I could to get her out of jail. Not taking a moment to think for a second that she took her phone with her because there was already someone else. As soon as she came out of jail the arguments continued. And I became desperate for answers. I began to work on myself and read as much as I could about verbal abuse, boundaries and narcissistic abuse. At this point I started to realize what I was dealing with. But I still couldn't get the strength to leave her. But what I did begin to do was establish some boundaries with her. I had read a book that said establish boundaries. Explain them only once. And if the boundaries are still crossed make sure you enforce them. The book also stated that I must be willing to accept the consequences of what happens after I set these boundaries. The consequences would be either the abuser begins to change his ways, or the abuser will leave. In my case, my ex did not have a license at the time, so I was driving her everywhere. My boundary became simple, if you insult me and we are at home you will have to make arrangements to get a ride to work or anywhere. Or if you are in my car, you will have to get out and walk. Simple. I thought. So one day while things were calm I decided to tell her about these new found boundaries calmly. She didn't respond, just nodded in agreement. Of course there was more and more instances of verbal abuse but this time around I had boundaries. And I made her get out of my car and walk. Numerous times. Because she would not stop. I was feeling stronger and proud of myself for finally sticking to my guns and making her walk after treating me this way. Until the last and final straw.

The grand discard

I woke up that morning and asked her if my outfit looked bad. Even though I had worn the outfit a few weeks prior and she had said she liked it, this time she said No something doesn't look right. I don't like it. So all I said was So, did you lie a few weeks ago when you said it looked good? And that is all it took for her to go off on a name calling rampage. Of course. So I told her calmly I'm sorry but you are going to have to make arrangements to get to work today. I'm not going to be called names. She immediately walked out and disappeared to work. And that day I experienced what many narcissistic abuse victims know as The Silent Treatment. I was ignored completely for over 8 hours that day. Not a word, text, email, phone call to see if I was alive. Nothing. It really hurt because all I wanted was an apology for the insults that morning. But I never got an apology. I got silence which was even worse. She completely detached from me like I didn't even exist. And this was someone who just vowed to cherish and love me until death do us part. At this point I was giving up. I was realizing that she was never going to change. And that not even my boundaries were going to change her. But I was changing. Little by little I was getting stronger. And come July 29 after another terrible verbal attack I decided to pack my belongings and leave to a Domestic Violence Shelter an hour away from home. My children were on vacation at my sister's house so I took this trip alone to clear my head and figure out what I wanted. But the nights were long and the pain was unbearable. This is someone I just married. I wanted more than anything to make this marriage work. I loved her so much. She will never know how much I loved her. Because I loved her more than myself. I handed this woman my life over on a silver platter and let her change everything I knew about love. I lost all self- respect in the process of loving her. And I invested too much time and energy to make this work. I wanted a return on my investment. I tried again to fix things. Because the codependent in me thought I could fix her. Or change her, or become the right person to make her stop insulting me. But I couldn't. And she couldn't. I came back two days later thinking that maybe we could still fix this. That maybe she loved me deep down enough to try and make this relationship work. I got nothing but more silence. I decided to go out with my friend that night to Karaoke. I remember I came home at 1am. Only to find my ex laying in my children's room. I asked her who she had spoken to that night. And she said her friends. I didn't believe or trust her anymore so I asked her to show me her phone and she showed it to me from a distance. Like when you are hiding something you don't want someone to see. Then she said that she deleted all her messages to her friends and that I didn't need to see any of them. Then I realized that she had texted a strange number that I had never seen before. I asked her who it was and she said it was a friend of hers who is married and was saved as a contact on her phone. I knew she was lying. I knew deep down this was the new object of her attention. The person I was getting the silent treatment over. The person who had no idea what she was about to get into. I asked her for hours that night who she was, and my ex refused to say a word. She said she would be out the next day. I knew in my heart that there was someone else. I know there was. And sure enough, just like that July 31st, 2015 my ex-wife decided to walk out of our marriage. Like we had not just gotten married two months before that. Like we had not promised to be together until death do us part. And just like that, I was discarded. Two months later, I saw pictures of her and her girlfriend at her friend's house. I knew at that moment my intuition did not fail me.

I can sit here and say blame my ex for everything but I choose not to. I had my part in this story as well. I am a codependent. But with that being just because I am a codependent, does not mean I don't deserve to be treated with respect. And now I can proudly say that if this had not happened, I probably would not have gotten into recovery from codependency. This ending was also the beginning to a new life for me. A life without verbal abuse. A life where I don't have to settle for pain anymore. Sometimes when you do not have the strength to leave someone toxic they get taken from you one way or the other. The most unbearable pain I have ever experienced was the pain of my narcissistic ex leaving me. But it has also been the pain that has set me free to find myself again, my voice, my self-love and my self-esteem. Because these things were buried deep inside me to make her happy. And I realize that in order for me to be happy I need to love myself over anybody else. I cannot keep putting myself in second place. Second place just doesn't work for me anymore. I didn't know what I deserved and how I deserved to be treated until someone came and treated me so poorly that I had no choice but to learn the hard way about the things I don't want. This relationship taught me that I cannot put the key to my happiness in someone else's pockets. And it taught me that I am never stuck. And that I do have choices. And just like I chose to stay as long as I did, I also could have made the choice to leave for good. But everything happens for a reason. And sometimes it takes a terrible situation to push you into your own recovery. And that is exactly what this relationship taught me. How to love myself.

The following 10 steps to healing from Narcissistic abuse have been created and tested by myself, for my own recovery from my very own abusive relationship. I have been to the darkest of sides of this abuse and I have found a specific set of things that have helped me tremendously in healing, feeling happier, stronger, and moving on with my life. I want you to know that this is possible. That there is truly hope after abuse. That there is life. Your life. And it can start whenever you make that decision to take your power back. I hope this list helps you and guides you into a new life. A life full of light, peace and love.

Step 1: Tell me who you are and what your boundaries are

From experience, I have to say that people will only treat us the way that we allow them to. A lack of boundaries allows a lack of respect. Only you can decide how you are going to allow people to treat you. Typically we struggle with boundaries due to a couple of different reasons. One of these reasons can be Codependency. Codependency stems from childhood trauma and living with dysfunctional and toxic people as a child. We are wired since childhood to believe that it is ok to be treated less than, or to feel that we are not worthy. This belief stays with us throughout our lives and turns into Codependency as adults. Making it impossible to choose healthy partners. Which is one of the reasons we stay in abusive and toxic situations far longer than we should. As codependents we have trouble enforcing and sticking to any boundaries we may set. We need to learn how to enforce our boundaries. We need to make our boundaries with the people in our lives who disrespect us and treat us as if we are not worthy. And we need to stop being afraid to walk away if they break our boundaries. We deserve to be treated with respect, all the time. And the way we can begin to do that weather you are still living with the abuser or not is to begin setting your boundaries. Here are some boundaries you may want to consider implementing in your own life. These boundaries have helped me tremendously in my healing journey.

I will not be verbally insulted, called names, put down or mocked. If you verbally abuse me you will have to leave, or I will leave and this relationship will be over. No excuses, no apologies. And you must be willing to enforce and follow through.

I will not allow any type of physical assaults in my home and I will not be made to feel unsafe in my home.

I will not allow drug abuse or any addictions in my home or near me.

You can act crazy and scream all you want but you will not do it around me, I will leave your presence if you act this way.

These are just some examples of some boundaries that have worked for me. However, you may want to add some to your own list that work for you. I suggest you pull out a sheet of paper and write some boundaries down. Keep this list where you can see it. Setting boundaries is life changing. The more you begin asserting your rights as an individual, the more self-confidence you will begin to feel. It is a chain reaction that will only take you higher in life. You will begin to feel stronger and more empowered the more boundaries you enforce.

Step 2: No Contact- Or limited Contact (Grey Rock) if you have children together.

This step is not for the faint at heart. This is probably going to be the hardest step and also the most important step in Recovering from Narcissistic abuse. The reason I suggest No Contact is because this is truly the way to gain some perspective and clarity on the reality of what you have just been through. You have just been through a devastating breakup with a narcissist and your entire world has been turned upside down. You are hurting, your pain is unbearable and you do not know how you are going to survive this. Well, No contact is going to be the anchor that keeps you afloat. There is no need to be in constant contact with somebody who has destroyed your heart and shattered your soul. People who truly care for you and love you do not just walk out and pretend like you never existed. Love does not hurt. Love does not verbally and mentally or physically abuse you. None of these instances are true love. No contact will give you the gift of your life back. It may seem and feel like you are going through withdrawal during these first couple of months. Love is an addiction. And we become trauma bonded with the abuser after many fights, arguments and traumatic episodes with them. So what happens is we feel like we cannot live without them. But the reality is we lived without them before we met them, and we can live again after them. By not communicating with them, you are giving yourself time to heal and recover. You are giving yourself the peace and mental clarity that you need to gain some perspective and get over this situation. You are protecting your heart. You are protecting your mind. You have been through enough abuse already. Give yourself this time to grow and move on from this experience. I understand many of you have children with the abuser, and in these instances the grey rock method is highly recommended. To grey rock means you ONLY communicate with the abuser when it has to do with your children that you share. You only share facts about the children. Nothing more, nothing less. No excuses. There is no more reasons to communicate with somebody who hurt you so deeply. Give yourself the gift of your life back. No contact means:

You block him/her on all social media such as Facebook, Twitter, Instagram, Email, Chat, anything and everything related to the internet.

You block all phone numbers, text messaging

You block all his friends and family

Basically you disappear from his/her radar. You are nowhere to be found on the planet when it comes to your narcissistic ex.

I say that No Contact is not for the faint at heart because it truly is not. It is the hardest thing I have ever done. I used to be the girl watching my exes Facebook page like a mad woman. I used to be the one responding to every crazy drunk call from my ex at 3 am, and responding to my ex's text messages projecting guilt onto me. And I will tell you what I learned from doing this. Every single time I responded or even read a text, I felt worse, sadder, more depressed, more devastated and I would hate myself for doing it. So it's a cycle that we must learn to break and practice the strictest form of self-control. I will leave you with this quote regarding No Contact.

Albert Einstein- "Insanity is doing the same thing over and over and expecting a different result."

Step 3: Practice Affirmations

Positive affirmations are truly a great way to begin changing the way you feel about yourself after an abusive relationship. It is one of the biggest changes I have made in my personal life after abuse. When

you are living with a verbally abusive lover, they begin to tell you

who you are. I know from my own experience I was called a dumb

cunt and worthless whore on a daily basis. So I began to believe

that it must be true. That I must be that awful because my ex said

so. And hearing this repeated to you on a daily basis is so damaging

to you that you begin to replay these tapes in your head over and

over until you begin to feel like you truly are worthless. A huge part

of healing from Narcissist and Verbal abuse is to realize that only

you can say who you are and nobody else has the right to tell you

who you are. By practicing positive self-esteem affirmations on a

daily basis. Repeating them to yourself as many times as you need

for them to begin becoming a part of your daily life. At first it may

feel weird to look at yourself in the mirror and repeat I am worthy. I

am beautiful. I am valuable. I deserve to be treated with respect. But

once you make this a daily practice it becomes second nature. And

if and when you do hear verbal abuse you will know deep down this

is not who you are and you will have or make no time for it. Only you

can determine your self-worth. Your abuser is not the dictator of

your worth. Take your life back into your own hands and begin

asserting yourself. Some affirmations that worked for me are listed below, but feel free to grab that piece of paper again and list your own personal affirmations. You can do this.

I am worthy.

I am valuable

My safety and security are within me.

I am beautiful just the way I am.

I am a good mother

I am strong

I am smart

I can do hard things

I can take good care of myself

I determine my worth

I do not need anybody to validate me

Step 5: Practice Extreme Self Care

A breakup with a Narcissist or Toxic Person will leave you feeling drained. Physically, mentally and emotionally you will feel like you just got ran over by a truck. You will not want to get out of bed, you will not want to eat or you will eat everything in sight, which was my case. You will not want to shower, or brush your hair, you just don't want to do anything. And after all why should you when you have suffered such a tremendous devastating blow? Well I'm going to tell you that taking care of yourself during this terrible time is crucial for surviving. Right now you should be in survival mode. Which means that you need to do whatever it takes to get through the day and function at your best. The only way you are going to get through this is if you practice self-care. Self-care is just daily rituals that you put into place to take care of yourself. Some examples of good self-care can be getting enough sleep, drinking enough water, taking a walk, eating 3 healthy meals a day, taking a shower, getting dressed out of your pajamas and forcing yourself to go outside and get some sunshine for a few minutes every day. You are still here, you are still breathing, you are still alive no matter how bad you feel right now. You are alive for a reason. You survived this for a reason. And you need to take good care of yourself because nobody else can do this for you. You need to take baby steps into your own healing and you can do this. One foot in front of the other. One day at a time. Take 10 minutes a day and do something that will make you feel better about yourself. Buy a new lipstick, get a new hairstyle, and try on a new blouse, anything that will help you create a feeling of well-being. This is crucial in your healing. It will empower you and make you feel better about yourself. You can do hard things. You can get through this.

Step 6: Find a hobby or renew old hobbies

I remember when my breakup with my narcissistic ex was recent I did not want to get out of bed. I remember there were so many days I called off work and just laid in bed, staring at the wall and crying. I let depression get the best of me. I let depression win so many times. But little by little I started to realize that I did not want to let my narcissistic ex continue to ruin my life. So I decided to take some action. This was also a suggestion from my good therapist at the time, which I highly recommend if you are feeling depressed or stuck in grief. There is nothing wrong with going to therapy and getting some help to help you move forward in your healing journey. One of the things I have always wanted to do was to write a book. I have always been fascinated by Self-help books and just the life of a writer in general. That is my passion. That is what I want to do with my life. That is what I am doing right now sitting here at 2:45am writing this very book. When I first got involved in my relationship with my ex, I had given up all of my hobbies in order to make my ex happy and be everywhere my ex was. I was a codependent cling on of the 5th kind. And this is not something I am proud to admit but I have then sought help and changed my ways with the help of Codependents Anonymous. It has truly changed my life. I no longer feel the need to throw out all my hobbies and interests out the window just because I am with somebody. You matter. And your interests matter. And in order to move on with your life you must seek out what makes you happy. Not your ex, but you. This is your life and you get to sit in the driver's seat now. This can be fun. You can find new hobbies you never even knew you enjoyed. There are so many things you can do. You can begin a sport, you can try art therapy coloring books which I love by the way, you can read, you can write, you can sing, you can travel, and you can go to meet ups with people who share similar interests as you. The sky is the limit here and you truly must pick things you enjoy doing just for you. The days of trying to make your abusive ex happy are over. These days are all about you. What old hobbies did you practice before your ex came along? Cultivate these hobbies again. Spend time doing fun things you love and in time you will see that you have begun to heal and recover because you have finally found yourself.

Step7: Don't be afraid to feel your feelings

Your feelings after a Narcissistic Relationship are going to be all over the place after the breakup. You are going to have days when you feel like you got this, that you can do this, that you are a badass bitch from hell and you are kicking ass and taking names. But then you are also going to have days where your ass is being kicked and all you can do is cry. Understand that both of these feelings are completely normal. If I can give you one piece of advice here is to not be afraid to feel whatever it is you feel. Feelings come and go, and we do not have to necessarily do anything about them except feel them, observe them passively. Because they will pass. I remember that I went through a rage phase where all I could think of was burning my ex's car down like Angela Bassett in Waiting to Exhale. Oh boy, I really wanted to re-create that scene. It lasted about a week or two. Pure rage, anger, at the life I lost, the love I lost, the wedding we had just experienced and to be dumped two months later for another supply. I was devastated, I was angry. I tried at first to put on a band-aid and pretend like I could easily get over what my ex did to me. But like Taylor Swift says Band-Aids don't fix Bullet Holes. So very true. I tried drinking and going out every single night after my ex left. Getting drunk, even worse, getting lost in my car at 3am drunk with no cell phone battery on the South Side of town. Not a fun experience. So I gave up drinking and partying. And then I tried a human band-aid. Another person so very fond of me, who loved bombed me so hard and put me on a pedestal. But that ended very quickly when I realized that person was you guessed it…another narcissist. So the moral of that story is, do not be afraid to sit with your feelings and feel whatever you need to feel. Know that the feeling will pass and you will reach a new level of acceptance. It takes time. And that's the worst of it. That unfortunately grief cannot be rushed. We all experience grief at our own pace and it is going to take as long as it takes. But you will come out stronger and wiser because of this. There are 5 stages of grief and you will go through all of them back and forth many times throughout this process. But one day you will reach acceptance, and on that day you will experience something beautiful. A peace like no other will overcome your heart and you will understand that everything happens for a reason. Even if that reason was so that you could find yourself again.

Step 8: Understand that you cannot control others

This is a very hard step to learn. We try so hard to fix other people who are damaged. Not realizing that in this world the only person we have control over is our self. We cannot change other people. And that is a hard reality to grasp. But you must understand that people never change because you want them to, or because you have made them see the light, or because they are hurting you, people do not change until they are ready to change on their own time. We have absolutely zero, none, no control over what another person does, says, doesn't do, feels or does not feel. We can only control our behavior, our feelings, and what we are willing to accept and tolerate from them. You can beg and cry all day and night till you are blue in the face. Trust me I did many times. I begged, I cried I hoped my ex would see how badly I was hurting from the verbal abuse. But that never happened. It was not acknowledged. My ex did not change. And there was no amount of crying or guilt trips I could impose to make my ex want to stop name calling or putting me down. The only thing we are left with is ourselves. We do have choices. We do not have to allow others to treat us in disrespectful ways. Life does not have to be so painful. We can choose to not engage. We can choose to respect ourselves and stay away from toxic people. We have that choice and that right. We have no business trying to control or change anybody else. But we do not have to tolerate abuse for one second. Once you realize that you cannot change your ex you will become ready to finally let go. To let go is to accept that this is who they are, this is who you are, and this is what you do not need to tolerate anymore. This is your life. Own it. This is something that I learned by going to Coda meetings and working the 12 steps with a sponsor. This is not for everybody but it is absolutely the root of my reasons for staying with abusive people. Codependency can sneak its way into your life and without you even realizing it, you are forgiving the unforgivable.

Step 9: Take time to be alone and find yourself again

I do not recommend by any means jumping into another relationship for at least a year or more after a relationship with a narcissist. The reason being, you need time to heal and recover inside and out. This time is crucial in understanding what has happened to you, educating yourself about narcissistic abuse, and learning to survive and take care of yourself on your own. This time is imperative and a sacred time for you. You must learn to become comfortable being alone, taking full responsibility for your choices and understanding the reasons why you stayed with an abuser. The reasons are different for everyone but some common reasons that many of us share include Codependency and Low Self Esteem. These are core issues that we must work on before jumping into another relationship. If we do not take this time to work on ourselves we will continue to seek out abusive and narcissistic partners. The chances of repeating the cycle are extremely higher if you do not take this time out to work on yourself and your childhood wounds. I recommend you begin by either finding a therapist who is trained in Narcissistic Abuse recovery, joining Coda.org to work on your Codependency Issues, joining an online support group or in person support group for abuse survivors, talking to others who have been through similar issues. You tube also has amazing channels on Codependency, Self-esteem and Narcissistic abuse recovery. I have sat in my bed many times night after night watching videos and becoming my own therapist. If you can afford therapy however, I highly recommend it. This time alone is your healing sanctuary. This time alone will help you understand and reflect on everything that has happened and on how you want your life to be from here on out. Take this time for yourself. Take some time off from dating and meeting men for the purpose of a relationship to focus on yourself and find out who you are, what you like, don't like, and what your deal breakers are from now on. You want to meet someone eventually from a place where you want to spend time with them, not from need. Because anytime we go into a relationship as a half and not a whole person, we will always settle because we need them. Don't make that mistake again. We do not have to settle for abuse ever.

Step 10: Educate Yourself and Others on Narcissistic Abuse

Now that you are empowered from taking care of yourself, I want you to research and educate yourself on Narcissistic abuse. This type of abuse goes unnoticed many times and there are so many people still suffering from it. It destroys lives. Narcissists are personality disordered individuals not mentally disordered. Meaning a mental disorder patient can seek treatment, yet a narcissist has these personality traits ingrained in him. It is his personality. Who he is, And you cannot change him. Learning about the phases of Narcissistic abuse is key to understand what you have been through and why no contact is key into breaking free from the trauma bonds. Understanding that you were only supply to the narcissist, as painful as that may be, you were a source not a person to them. Which is why they feel no empathy or compassion when they hurt you. These people do not feel bad because in their mind they do not believe they have done anything wrong. They believe you deserved to be punished for not going along with their plans. A Narcissist will never feel true remorse. Any attempts to apologize are only to continue receiving whatever supply you are giving them. Or to continue abusing you on their terms. They will use you for supply until they have found someone else who can give them new supply. Then they will discard you with no remorse, no guilt. Supply to a narcissist means anything you are providing to them, that can mean validation, sex, car rides, a house, money, food, emotional support, or just feeding their ego. Once they have used you and you have nothing more in you to give, they will sense it and move on to another target willing to give everything for them not knowing what they are about to get into. Because the narcissist will never change.

The only thing that changes is the victim and the mask they wear. Now that you are out of the relationship, when you start to feel sad about everything that has happened, find an article online about narcissism, read this book, find a video, anything that will confirm to you that you are not crazy, that you are in fact a survivor of narcissistic abuse. Understand that you did not know better at the time and forgive yourself for what you did not know. But now you are armed with knowledge. And knowledge will set you free. Another thing that has helped along with educating myself on narcissism has been sharing that information with others who are still suffering from the abuse. The more people I meet in my support group that I created because I had no supportive family or friends at the time, the more I feel like I am a part of a bigger plan. And now I don't feel alone anymore because there are so many other woman and men going through this. The support I find online has been a life saver. We are truly there for each other and have become a family. Education and sharing that knowledge with others will add so many blessings to your own healing journey. You will begin to rise and empower yourself. You will begin to trust yourself. You will learn that there was nothing you could do to stop this person. And that you do have choices now. You can choose to stay away. You can spot the red flags now. You can choose to say no. You are in control now. It's your life and you can be happy again.

There are some walks you have to take alone in life

There comes a time in your life where you have to decide to put yourself first. Narcissistic abuse leaves you feeling completely devastated and questioning everything you knew about yourself. You must learn to forgive yourself for the things you did not know until now. You have some really amazing qualities in you that you must find again. The narcissist did everything in their power to make you forget about these qualities. Or as in many of our cases childhood trauma also caused us to forget our value and worth. But these qualities are still in you. You must be courageous and find your way back to you. Working on yourself and taking this time to heal these deep wounds is the only way. Time spent reflecting on who you are and you who will no longer be. Time to grieve the horrible pain they left us with. You must decide that this is your life and that they can no longer control your happiness. Your happiness lies within. True happiness comes from knowing ourselves, and taking the time to appreciate every single thing about ourselves. That takes time. And so does getting over these relationships. Time really does heal but it takes time. Be gentle with yourself. You are doing the best you can with the cards you were dealt. One day you will begin to see that this happened not because something was wrong with you, but because there were so many things that were right about you. Such as your compassion, empathy, kind heart and caring soul. These are qualities that you must hold on to and not ever let anyone take them away from you. There are just some walks in life you will have to take alone to find these things again.

In conclusion:

These are just some key things that have helped me in my own person healing and recovery from Narcissistic Abuse. However, I do want to mention, that recovery is not the same for everyone. Everyone is different and has their own unique healing journey ahead of them. I wanted to write this as a starting point to lead you in the right direction, towards a happy healthier state of mind, and a peaceful life full of joy, serenity, and most importantly a journey of self-love. Without learning to truly love ourselves and put ourselves first, we will continue to allow others to dictate our value and worth. Only we have the right to dictate that for ourselves. Never put the key to your happiness in someone else's pocket. You deserve to be treated with the utmost respect all the time. A narcissist will never understand this concept. They will never understand because they feel justified in treating you this way when things do not go their way. It's time to get off the Supply Party Train and get back on track as driver of your own life. You have already taken a giant step towards healing or else you would not be reading this book. Continue with this momentum and pretty soon a year will pass and you will look back on what the narcissist put you through and you will feel nothing but relief. Relief that you no longer have to be treated that way, relief because now you are armed with the truth of who they are and who they can never be. Starting today I want you to make a promise to yourself that you will never let another person dictate who you are or treat you in any other way but with respect and dignity. Starting today promise yourself that you will not settle for the crumbs of a narcissists attention but only seek out loving, gentle, kind, and compassionate human beings to spend your time with. But above all promise yourself that you will be all these things for yourself first, and you will love yourself above all others and treat yourself with love, every single day.

References:

The following is a list of the many websites, books and phone numbers that have helped me tremendously in my own recovery. Knowledge is empowerment and I want to share with you the resources to empower yourself.

Verbal And Narcissist Abuse Support Group-My own Facebook Group I created to begin my own recovery journey and to help as many people as I can in their own healing journeys.

Narcissist Abuse Survivors Facebook Group

PhsycopathFree.com

Coda.org-Codependents Anonymous Website

Thehotline.org-National Domestic Violence Website

Selfcarehaven.wordpress.com-Great blog on Narcissistic abuse and self-care

Narcissist Support YouTube Channel

Ross Rosenberg-YouTube Channel

Self-Care Haven YouTube Channel

Lisa Romano-YouTube Channel

Spartan Life Coach-YouTube Channel

Books:

Codependent No More-Melody Beattie

Psychopath Free- Jackson Mackenzie

The Language of Letting Go- Melody Beattie

The verbally abusive relationship-Patricia Evans

The survivors quest-Healing Journey

National Domestic Violence Hotline- 1-800-799-7233

You Must Love Yourself First

Starting today I want you to know that a life of hope and happiness is possible. And that this abuse does not define who you are. I want you to give it everything you got and reach out for your own recovery. I want you to put yourself first again. And to remind yourself in weak moments that you deserve to be treated with respect at all times, no matter what. No matter what your childhood trauma may be, no matter what your personal defects of character may be, no matter what your insecurities are, you still deserve to be treated with respect. I want you to never settle to be treated any less. I hope my story and my steps to healing will help you in your own recovery and at the very least serve as a starting point in your own healing. Our healing journey is and will be unique to all of us, but one thing we do share in common is that we have all been touched by a Narcissist and that we are all now survivors. My wish for you is that you find the strength, hope, healing, peace, light and love in your journey back to self.

Made in the USA
San Bernardino, CA
13 December 2016